# SPIES,

## DOUBLE AGENTS,

## and

## Traitors

### BY SUSAN K. MITCHELL

THE SECRET WORLD OF SPIES

Enslow Publishers, Inc.
40 Industrial Road
Box 398
Berkeley Heights, NJ 07922
USA    http://www.enslow.com

## For my wonderful parents, Robbie & Dub

**Library of Congress Cataloging-in-Publication Data**

Mitchell, Susan K.
 Spies, double agents, and traitors / Susan K. Mitchell.
  p. cm. — (The secret world of spies)
 Includes bibliographical references and index.
 Summary: "Discusses double agents and traitors throughout history, such as Benedict Arnold,
Dusan Popov, Kim Philby, and Robert Hanssen, and includes information on becoming a spy catcher
(counterintelligence agent)"—Provided by publisher.
 ISBN 978-0-7660-3711-3
 1. Spies—Juvenile literature. 2. Espionage—Juvenile literature. 3. Spies—Biography—
Juvenile literature. 4. Traitors—Juvenile literature. I. Title.
 UB270.5.M578 2011
 327.12—dc22

                    2010006178

Paperback ISBN 978-1-59845-351-5

Printed in China

052011 Lake Book Manufacturing, Inc., Melrose Park, IL

10 9 8 7 6 5 4 3 2 1

**To Our Readers:** We have done our best to make sure all Internet Addresses in this book were
active and appropriate when we went to press. However, the author and the publisher have no
control over and assume no liability for the material available on those Internet sites or on other
Web sites they may link to. Any comments or suggestions can be sent by e-mail to comments
@enslow.com or to the address on the back cover.

**Illustration Credits:** Al Stephenson / Reuters / Landov, p. 42; © Elena Korenbaum / iStockphoto.com,
p. 7 (bottom); FBI, pp. 3, 45; The Granger Collection, New York, pp. 10, 15; Hulton Archive / Getty Images,
pp. 18, 33; Library of Congress, pp. 8, 13; © MGM / Everett Collection, p. 22; Paul J. Richards / AFP / Getty
Images, p. 40; Popperfoto / Getty Images, p. 29; Reuters / Landov, p. 44; Robert F. Sargent / U.S. Coast
Guard, p. 25; Shutterstock.com, p. 4; Time & Life Pictures / Getty Images, p. 38; Tim Ockenden / Press
Association Images, p. 23; © Trinity Mirror / Mirrorpix / Alamy, p. 31; U.S. Army Center of Military History,
pp. 7 (top), 26; U.S. Navy, p. 27.

**Cover Illustration:** Mehau Kulyk / Photo Researchers, Inc. (background); Shutterstock.com (dark
silhouettes in front of Earth, lower right corner).

# CONTENTS

# Chapter 1

# Nothing Is What It Seems

The basic skill needed for spying is usually lying. Spies pretend to be something they are not. They lie and do whatever is necessary to complete their missions. Simply put, spies are often not to be trusted. Double agents take that to a different level.

Double agents are spies who pretend to work for one country or agency. In reality, they work for the enemy country or agency instead. For example, Russian

KGB agents would pose as American agents. They get jobs working for the Central Intelligence Agency (CIA). But what they are actually doing is finding out CIA secrets. Then they give those secrets to the KGB.

Some double agents may be traitors. A traitor spies on his or her country for the enemy. Other double agents may agree to spy for the enemy only after they have been captured. It may be the only way they can avoid death. Whatever the double agent's reason, this type of spying plays one side against the other. It is the ultimate double cross, and the price for betrayal can be high. Many double agents face prison or death if caught.

## Treason Has a Name

One name in spying has become synonymous with the word traitor. That name is Benedict Arnold. He is one of the most infamous double agents in American history. He had many reasons for turning against his country. Some reasons were revenge; some were pride. Either way, he ended up working for the British forces during the American Revolution.

In his early military career, Benedict Arnold was a trusted army officer. He was well liked by General George Washington. He was not, however, well liked by many men in the Continental Congress, the

# Unlucky 13

General James Wilkinson was a double agent. He was known as Agent 13.

**G**eneral James Wilkinson was an American army officer. He was also a double agent and a traitor. Wilkinson spied on the United States for Spain. He was known as Agent 13. His most famous plot involved Aaron Burr, who was not some low-level military officer. He was the vice president under President Thomas Jefferson!

Burr was plotting to gain control of parts of the American south. These included Louisiana, Texas, and part of Mexico. He wanted to create his own country, separate from the United States. Burr even formed his own army. Wilkinson helped him in this plot while working for Spain. When Burr failed to support Wilkinson, however, the double agent exposed Burr's plans.

governing body of the United States during the American Revolution. They often blamed him when battles failed. Arnold felt he was being treated unfairly. His anger continued to grow over the years.

By May 1779, Arnold decided to help the British. Driven by revenge, Arnold met secretly with others who were still loyal to England. His main contact was British officer Major John Andre.

The name and face of Benedict Arnold will forever be linked with the word traitor.

Spies, DOUBLE AGENTS, and Traitors

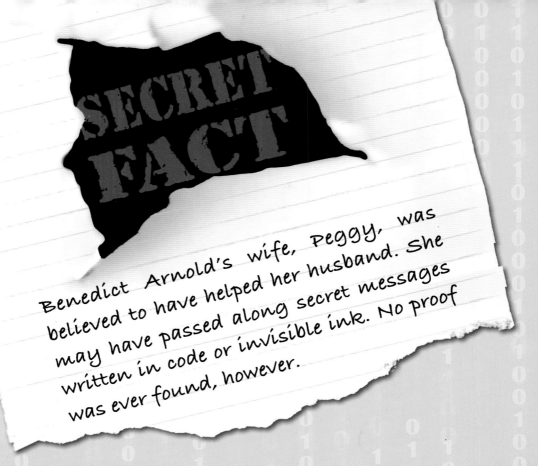

Benedict Arnold's wife, Peggy, was believed to have helped her husband. She may have passed along secret messages written in code or invisible ink. No proof was ever found, however.

## Turning Coats

Soon, Benedict Arnold was supplying Andre with information. He told him about troop locations. He also gave Andre information about supplies and weapons. However, Arnold had an even bigger plan in mind. He wanted to turn over West Point to the British. West Point was considered one of the best American military forts.

Arnold received an appointment to West Point. He was given command of the fort in August 1780.

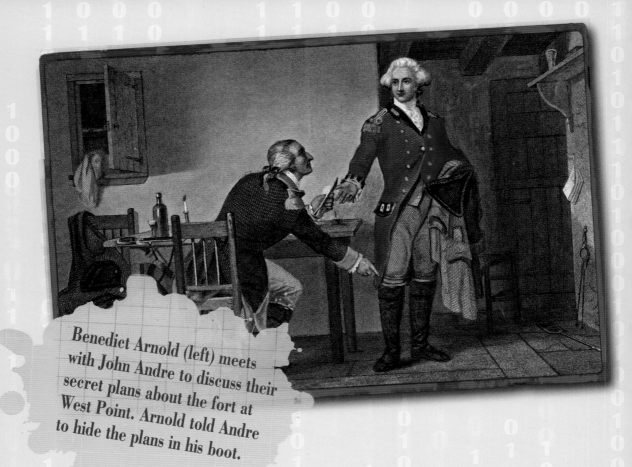

Benedict Arnold (left) meets with John Andre to discuss their secret plans about the fort at West Point. Arnold told Andre to hide the plans in his boot.

Right away, he began sending information to the British. Arnold secretly worked to weaken the fort's defenses, too. He did everything possible to make West Point easy for the British to capture.

Everything seemed to be going according to plan. That is, until Andre was captured. American soldiers found letters and other important documents in his pockets. They were from Arnold. The plot had been exposed! Benedict Arnold was officially a traitor.

Arnold found out about Andre's capture. He had to escape. He ran and joined up with the British troops for protection. Andre was not so lucky. He was hanged by American Revolution forces. Arnold eventually escaped to England. He lived there until he died in 1801. To this day, he is most known as an American traitor.

# A High Price to Pay

Double agents or traitors are often paid large sums of money for their services. Getting caught, however, can be a far higher price to pay. Sometimes it may mean life in prison. Traitors could also lose their home, money, and all of their belongings.

In many countries, the punishment for treason is death! The death may be particularly gruesome and violent. This is because treason is seen as such a dangerous crime. Double agents are risking their lives when they decide to become a traitor.

# Chapter 2

# Dancing With Danger

**E**spionage can be an art. It is the art of creating another personality. It is the art of living a lie. Double agents have to be very good actors to convince each side that they are working for them. It requires talent and charm.

Margaretha Zelle was just such a spy. She is quite possibly the most famous female spy in history. She was not known by the name Margaretha, however. She is best known by the name Mata Hari.

A photo of Margaretha Zelle, better known as the spy Mata Hari.

After a very bad marriage, Margaretha left her home in the Netherlands. She moved to Paris, France. It was there that she began to work as an entertainer and dancer. She even claimed to be an Indonesian princess. She also told people she was a trained temple dancer. Margaretha wore exotic jeweled costumes. She became very popular around France. She then took the stage name, Mata Hari, which means the "eye of dawn."

Dancing was not Mata Hari's first job in France. At first, she worked as a circus horse rider.

## Wickedly Charming

Mata Hari's career as a spy did not start right away. As she grew more popular, she became friends with some very important people. Many of them were rich. Some had a lot of power in France. Others were high-level German military members. Mata Hari even had a relationship with the German crown prince.

Because Mata Hari was still a citizen of the Netherlands, she could come and go across international borders with little question. None of this was important until World War I. It was then that her great beauty, charm, and travels caught the eye of several

Mata Hari began working for many different countries during World War I. But her spying activities were a mystery.

intelligence agencies. They became suspicious that she was a spy. Worse yet, it was believed she might be a double agent.

No country was sure who Mata Hari worked for. When stopped by the British, she claimed to be a French spy. She said she was spying on the Germans. The French agencies were suspicious that she was actually working for the Germans. They sent her to Spain to spy on the Germans anyway. Since becoming Mata Hari, she had woven so many lies that it was impossible to tell to which country she was loyal. Mata Hari was a mystery.

## The Kiss of Death

Eventually, the British forces claimed to find proof that Germany had paid Mata Hari for information against the French. It is still unclear if the claims were true. French intelligence also intercepted a message from the Germans. It was a coded message. However, it was in a code that the French had already broken.

The messages claimed that a spy by the code name of H-21 had given them very helpful information. From the other information in the messages, the French claimed that H-21 was none other than Mata Hari! When she finally came back to Paris from Spain, Mata Hari was arrested.

# Mirroring Mata Hari

World War II had its own female double agent. Vera Schalburg went by many names. She was also a dancer in France. Like Mata Hari, she used her beauty and charm to find out secrets. Vera also had no loyalty. She was a notorious double agent.

She spied on the Russian resistance for the Soviets. She spied on the Soviets for the Russian resistance. She spied on the British and Soviets for the Germans. She even spied on the Germans for the British. Vera was every bit as mysterious as Mata Hari. Like her counterpart, Vera was eventually arrested. Strangely, she did not stand trial. By the end of World War II, Vera had vanished without a trace.

Mathilde Carre, also known as the Cat, worked as a double agent for the Germans.

# Clever Cat

Women have made some of the best spies in history. The simple fact that they are women seemed to help them avoid any suspicion. Mathilde Carre was another famous female double agent.

Little about French-born Mathilde signaled "spy." She was very quiet. She was educated. She was even a teacher. During World War II, however, Mathilde began to work as a French spy. Her code name was the "Cat."

When the Germans captured her, she agreed to turn double agent. She then began to spy on her native France for Germany. She also spied on the British. Eventually, the Cat used the last of her nine lives. Mathilde was captured in England. She was sent to France and sentenced to death. But her sentence was changed to life in prison.

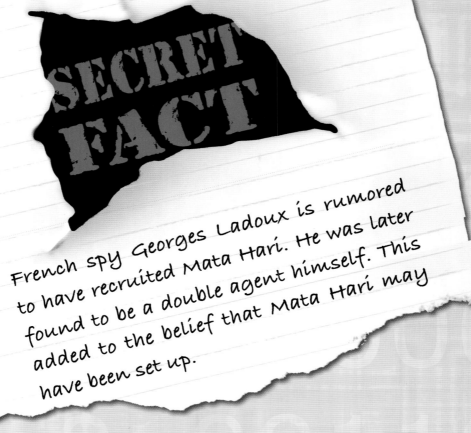

French spy Georges Ladoux is rumored to have recruited Mata Hari. He was later found to be a double agent himself. This added to the belief that Mata Hari may have been set up.

In 1917, the French government tried Mata Hari for treason. She was accused of being a double agent working for Germany. She was sentenced to death by firing squad. On October 15, she faced twelve guns without a blindfold. It was even rumored that she blew a kiss to the firing squad before she was shot to death. It was the end for Mata Hari but just the beginning of her legend as a double agent.

# More Than Child's Play

One part of a double agent's job is to find out secrets. That agent needs to give false information to the enemy. Giving up secrets makes it look like he or she is truly working for the enemy agency. What the double agent is really doing is throwing them off track.

The information has to be believable. It cannot look like it may be a lie. Double agents cannot afford to blow their cover. Dusan Popov was a double agent who was very good at this. He was born in Yugoslavia but spoke fluent German. Popov had several high-level German friends, too. Eventually, he agreed to be a German spy during World War II.

It looked like Popov was a loyal German spy. But there was something the Germans did not know. Popov hated the Nazis. He only agreed to be a spy so he could become a double agent and work against the Germans!

**SECRET FACT**

Popov was friends with Ian Fleming, the creator of the fictional spy James Bond 007. It is believed that Popov was the inspiration for the 007 character.

Dusan Popov may have been the inspiration for the famous fictional spy James Bond. In this photo, actor Daniel Craig portrays James Bond in the movie *Quantum of Solace.*

## Toying With Treason

Immediately after signing on as a Nazi spy, Popov contacted the MI5. This was the British secret intelligence agency. He offered to become a double agent for them. He was assigned a code name by the MI5. Popov would become famously known as Tricycle.

Tricycle was famously elegant. He was handsome and charming. This allowed him to move with ease through German circles. He gave the Germans what were believed to be British secrets. In reality, the secrets were carefully created by the British themselves. They were believable enough to make Tricycle look like an effective spy to the Germans.

In true spy fashion, Tricycle often used elaborate spy techniques to pass along the messages. He used invisible ink on postcards. He also used microdots—extremely small film images. It was all in an effort to keep the Germans believing that Tricycle was on their side. It worked like a charm!

Several documents were found in Tricycle's file, including his forumla for invisible ink.

# And the Code Name Is . . .

In Disney Pixar's movie, *The Incredibles*, Elastigirl tells her children, "Your identity is your most precious possession. Protect it." This is true in real life for spies. That is why they often have code names. These names can protect them from harm, or even death.

Double agents Garbo and Brutus both worked with Tricycle during World War II. Other well-known agents had names like Zig Zag and Snow. Two Norwegian spies were called Mutt and Jeff after some popular cartoon characters. The real names of many of these agents are still unknown to this day.

## Tipping the Balance

In 1944, Tricycle was part of his most important mission yet. It was called Operation Fortitude. It also led to a shift of power in World War II. Tricycle sent more false information to the Germans. Several other double agents did the same thing. They all sent

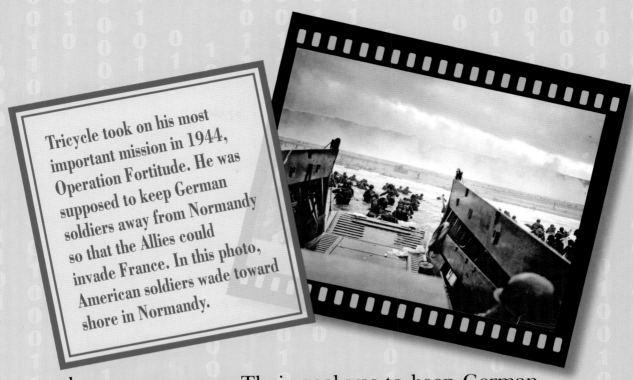

Tricycle took on his most important mission in 1944, Operation Fortitude. He was supposed to keep German soldiers away from Normandy so that the Allies could invade France. In this photo, American soldiers wade toward shore in Normandy.

the same message. Their goal was to keep German forces away from Normandy, France.

The false information was extremely believable. The Nazi military had no reason to suspect Tricycle or the other agents. Since they were all relaying the same information, it seemed even more accurate. The beaches at Normandy were left almost completely unguarded by Nazi troops.

British, American, and other Allied forces were able to invade Normandy with relative ease except for a few bloody battles. They took the Nazi troops by surprise. It helped the Allies push the Nazis out of France. The invasion would have been very difficult to do without the help of double agents like Tricycle.

Allied soldiers storm the beaches of Normandy during the D-Day invasion. Double agents like Tricycle helped make the invasion more successful.

## SECRET FACT

Popov never took money from the British MI5. He claimed that helping defeat the Nazis was payment enough. Plus, he was paid a great deal by the Germans themselves.

# Information Unheeded

In 1941, the Germans sent Tricycle to the United States. He had been given a list of targets on which he was to gather information. One of those targets was Pearl Harbor, an important navy base in Hawaii.

Tricycle passed along this information to the Federal Bureau of Investigation (FBI). For some reason, FBI director J. Edgar Hoover did not act on this key piece of information. The Japanese attacked Pearl Harbor in December of that same year.

The battleship *Arizona* is sunk during the Japanese attack on Pearl Harbor.

# High-Ranking Spy

**S**ome spies turn double agent for the excitement. Others do it for the money. There are also those who never take a single penny. They decide to become double agents because of their political beliefs. If a spy truly believes in the ways of a certain government, he or she may agree to work for a country that has those same beliefs. That may even mean betraying his or her own country.

That is how the Soviet Union found many of their double agents. Communism was the Soviet Union's form of government before the late 1900s. It was different from the government in the United States. During the 1930s, many double agents liked the idea of Communism.

That is especially true of Kim Philby. It led him to become one of the most successful double agents in history. Philby was a college student at Cambridge in England. He and four friends believed in Communist ideas. Together, they created the Cambridge Five spy ring.

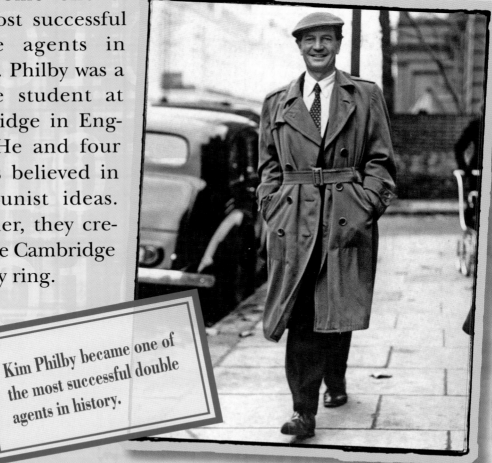

Kim Philby became one of the most successful double agents in history.

Kim Philby's real name was Harold Adrian Russell Philby. He was called Kim after a character in a Rudyard Kipling novel.

## Rising Through the Ranks

Philby began his spy career posing as a journalist. He was working undercover for the Soviets to spy on his British homeland. In 1940, he landed a job with the British secret services called the SIS. It was the perfect position to be in as a double agent. He was on the inside now. Philby would have access to even more information to send to the Soviets.

Over the next few years, Philby received promotions to higher positions. In 1944, he schemed his way to the head of the SIS Section IX department.

Kim Philby (right) began his spy career posing as a journalist. But he got a job with the British SIS and moved up the ranks. All this time, he gave British secrets to the Soviets.

This was the agency's anti-Soviet department. Philby had more access than ever. He now knew which Soviet agents were, in reality, spying for England. He also had access to top secret documents. Philby gave it all to the Soviets.

Over the years, Philby had relied on a few of his old Cambridge pals. Two of them were Guy Burgess and Donald Maclean. In 1950, both were found to be passing weapons secrets to the Soviets. To escape punishment, both men defected to the Soviet Union.

# XX Marks the Spy

During World War II, the British MI5 agency decided to use double agents to their fullest advantage. They created the Double Cross, or XX, System. This agency branch was in charge of creating double agents to spy for the British.

They used German spies, who had been captured. They also used German spies that had surrendered themselves. The XX System was responsible for providing the false information that the double agents sent back to the Germans.

Kim Philby was part of the Cambridge Five. Four members of the spy ring are seen here, clockwise from top left: Anthony Blunt, Donald Maclean, Philby, and Guy Burgess.

# A Hero for the Enemy

It was the beginning of the end for Kim Philby. His relationship to Burgess and Maclean was well known. Philby fell under suspicion. He was asked to resign from the SIS. He was questioned several times. But no proof was ever found to say he was a double agent. Philby was rehired, fired, and questioned many other times. Each time, like the master spy he was, he lied his way out of being caught.

As the years passed, Philby grew more careless. He often drank too much and said things he should not. In 1962, Flora Solomon, a woman who Philby had tried to recruit as a spy for the Soviets in the 1930s, gave information about him to the British. Philby was once again under suspicion.

He knew there was no way out this time. His only hope was to defect to the Soviet Union, which he did in 1963. There, he was seen as a national hero. No one knows how many British agents may have been killed because of the information Philby gave to the Soviets. He also passed along important secrets from the American CIA. These actions made Philby one of the most notorious double agents in British history.

Spies, DOUBLE AGENTS, and Traitors

# A Tangled Web of Lies

If the life of a double agent sounds confusing, imagine the life of Agnes Smedley. Throughout the 1900s, she spied for many different countries. She spied for the Soviet Union. Agnes also spied for the Chinese Communists. She even spied for India. Agnes was loyal to no country. The side she was on usually depended on the man she was dating at the time. She was captured and jailed several times.

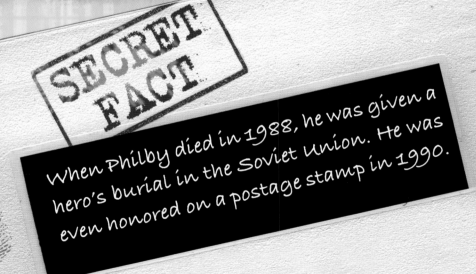

**SECRET FACT**

When Philby died in 1988, he was given a hero's burial in the Soviet Union. He was even honored on a postage stamp in 1990.

# In Too Deep

The life of a double agent is full of danger. Spies try to be careful to avoid it at any cost. Many of the things that can turn spies into double agents also cause them to quit being careful. Greed can cause double agents to take greater risks. Pride can cause double agents to think they are uncatchable. These and other reasons can make double agents careless.

When spies get careless, they may get caught. It may end up being the lies told to their loved ones that destroy them. That was ultimately what happened to one of history's most recent double agents, Robert Hanssen. His greed led him to take very dangerous risks. It was his carelessness that eventually caused his capture.

Robert Hanssen's career in espionage began very innocently in 1976. He started out with the FBI. In 1979, Hanssen moved to a FBI unit that tracked Soviet spy activity. It did not take long, however, for him to figure out there was much money to be made as a double agent.

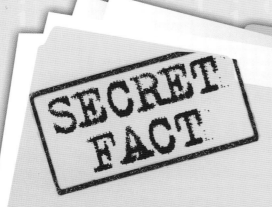

The Soviets had not one but two double agents during the 1980s. Notorious double agent Aldrich Ames was betraying the CIA at the same time that Robert Hanssen was betraying the FBI.

Aldrich Ames was a traitor to the United States. The FBI found this note from Ames to a Soviet KGB agent in Ames's trash can.

Spies, DOUBLE AGENTS, and Traitors

# Everyday People

Many double agents do not start out as spies at all. They do not work for intelligence agencies. They are regular people with regular jobs. These agents may have had a brush with the law. To avoid being punished, they may agree to become a spy. Iyman Faris was one such double agent. He was a U.S. citizen but loyal to al-Qaeda. Faris worked as a truck driver. He was involved in a terrorist plot to blow up the Brooklyn Bridge in New York. When confronted by the FBI, he agreed to be a double agent. Eventually, he was tried and jailed for his involvement with al-Qaeda.

## Switching Sides

Many double agents are recruited or turned by the enemy agency. But Robert Hanssen did not wait for the Soviets to come to him. He went straight to them! Hanssen offered to give the Soviets information in exchange for money. Money seemed to be his main motivation.

The ID and business card of former FBI agent Robert Hanssen.

Throughout the late 1970s and the early 1980s, Hanssen sold huge amounts of FBI secrets to the Soviets. He revealed other Soviet double agents who were working for the United States. Many of those agents ended up being killed by the Soviets. Hanssen repeatedly handed over information while asking for huge sums of money in return.

Hanssen's wife, Bonnie, began to get suspicious of her husband because of that money. On more than

one occasion, she found mysterious stashes of cash. Hanssen lied to her about where he got the money. It did not ease her suspicions. Bonnie's sister told her brother about what happened. He was an FBI agent, too. Hanssen's lies were catching up with him.

## The Hunt for a Betrayer

In 1990, Hanssen's brother-in-law told the FBI that they should investigate. For some reason, nothing was ever done. Hanssen continued to betray his country in secret. By the mid-1990s, it was becoming clear to intelligence agencies in the United States that they had a serious problem. They knew they had a double agent in their ranks. Even worse, it looked like they may have two of them.

In 1994, CIA double agent Aldrich Ames was caught. However, the Russians were still finding out secrets about the United States. They knew there must be another double agent still on the loose. The FBI and CIA teamed up to find out who it was. All the while, Hanssen worked under the false name Ramon Garcia. He boldly approached the Russians with information to sell. This time, he met them in person. Hanssen began taking bigger and bigger risks.

Aldrich Ames on his way to court after being arrested in 1994. Even after Ames's arrest, the FBI and CIA knew there was still a traitor working against them.

Hanssen's luck eventually ran out. He had taken one risk too many. His voice was recognized on a tape. A Russian double agent gave the tape to the FBI. The FBI knew that they had found their man. In 2001, they followed Hanssen to a dead-drop site and arrested him on the spot. Today, Hanssen is serving a life sentence in a high-security prison. He will never be up for parole.

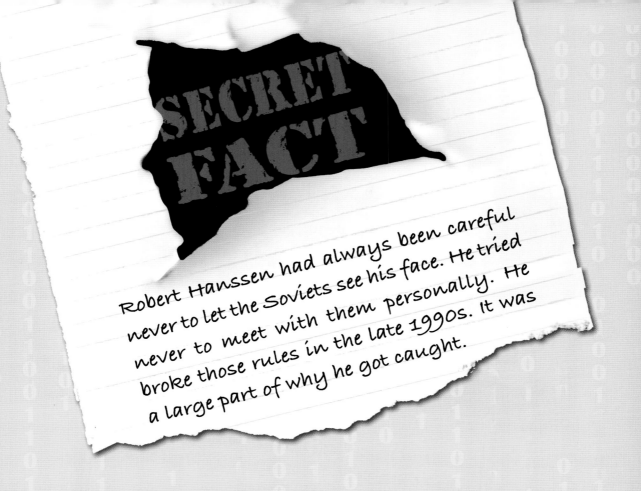

SECRET FACT

Robert Hanssen had always been careful never to let the Soviets see his face. He tried never to meet with them personally. He broke those rules in the late 1990s. It was a large part of why he got caught.

## Double the Trouble

It is clear throughout history that there are many reasons why spies may become double agents. They might do it for excitement or love. Money is usually a major factor. They may do it for their beliefs. No matter what the reason, a double agent commits a huge act of betrayal.

Some spies become double agents for the money. Robert Hanssen certainly did. This package of $50,000 was found at the dead-drop site used by Hanssen.

What is also true is that for most of them that betrayal ends badly. They are almost always captured. Many face death. The others face a life in prison. Some lose everything they have. In the end, the life of a double agent is often nothing more than double the trouble.

Spies, DOUBLE AGENTS, and Traitors

# SPIES

## like

## Who?

## BECOMING A SPY CATCHER

An FBI agent in training class.

Becoming a double agent is not the best career path for a person. Catching double agents, however, is big business. Spy catchers are called counterintelligence agents. Their job is to find double agents before they can do too much damage. Many government, military, and civilian agencies hire these spy catchers.

To apply to be an FBI spy catcher, a person must be between twenty-three and thirty-seven years old. A four-year college degree is required. He or she must apply to the counterintelligence program. FBI special agents train for twenty-one weeks. The training is very intense. Once the agents pass the training, they will start out making a salary somewhere between $61,000 and $69,000 per year.

# Glossary

**agency**—An intelligence organization.

**al-Qaeda**—A major Islamic terrorist organization.

**dead drop**—A secret spot where a spy leaves information or items for another spy or agency.

**defect**—To abandon one's own country to live in another country.

**espionage**—The act of spying.

**fluent**—To speak or write in a language correctly and with ease.

**traitor**—A person who betrays his or her country.

**treason**—The act of betraying one's country.

## Books

Burgan, Michael. **Spies and Traitors: Stories of Masters of Deception.** Mankato, Minn.: Capstone Press, 2010.

Gifford, Clive. **Spies Revealed.** New York: Atheneum Books for Young Readers, 2008.

Gilbert, Adrian. **Secret Agents.** Richmond Hill, Ontario: Firefly Books, 2009.

Martin, Michael. **Spy Skills.** Mankato, Minn.: Capstone Press, 2008.

Stewart, James. **Spies & Traitors.** North Mankato, Minn.: Smart Apple Media, 2009.

## Internet Addresses

Central Intelligence Agency (CIA): Kids' Page
<https://www.cia.gov/kids-page/index.html>

Federal Bureau of Investigation (FBI): Kids' Page
<http://www.fbi.gov/fun-games/kids/kids>

Spy Technology: Dialogue for Kids
(Idaho Public Television)
<http://idahoptv.org/dialogue4kids/season4/spy/index.cfm>

# Index